M000094557

40 Wonderful Blend & Digraph Poems

A Delightful Collection of Poems With an Easy-to-Use Lesson Plan to Help Young Learners Build Key Phonics Skills

compiled by Shelley Grant and Dana Haddad

NEW YORK • TORONTO • LONDON • AUCKLAND • SYDNEY
MEXICO CITY • NEW DELHI • HONG KONG • BUENOS AIRES

Teaching *Resources*

To my family, who fills my life with poetry.

–S.G.

To my family, friends, students, and colleagues who help make every day a poetic adventure.

–D.H.

Contents

Introduction...4

Using This Book...5

BR-
Brushes..8
Brooms...9

CH-
Cheers for Cherry Cake..............10
Chick, Chick, Chatterman...........11

CL-
The Click Clacker Machine.........12
Clown Class................................13

CR-
Crazy Crying Cats......................14
There Was a Crooked Man.........15

DR-
Dragon Dream...........................16
Raindrops..................................17

FL-
A Flea and a Fly in a Flue...........18
If I Could Fly...............................19

GR-
Grandma's Going to
the Grocery Store.......................20
Grasshopper Green....................21

PH-
Eletelephony.............................22
Phoebe's Phase.........................23

SH-
She Sells Seashells....................24
Shirley Shepherd.......................25

SK-
Skipping....................................26
Skyscraper.................................27

SL-
Icy...28
The Slow, Sleepy Sloth.............29

SN-
Snuggles the Snake...................30
The Snail...................................31

SP-
Spaghetti! Spaghetti!................32
Spin, Spider, Spin!....................33

SQU-
Showers....................................34
A Squirmy Squid.......................35

ST-
Rhyme.......................................36
Stella's Seed.............................37

SW-
In the Park................................38
My Sweet...................................39

TH-
Mice..40
There's a Hole in the Bucket..41

TR-
Troll Pal....................................42
Trick or Treat............................43

TW-
Twins...44
Twin Town.................................45

WH-
What Is Pink?............................46
White Sheep..............................47

Blend & Digraph Word Lists........48

Introduction

Welcome to *40 Wonderful Blend & Digraph Poems!*

> **blend:** a combination of letters in which each letter retains a separate sound (for example, *cr* as in *cry*, *fl* as in *flag*, *st* as in *stop*).
>
> **digraph:** a combination of letters that creates a sound different from the sound made by either letter (*ch* as in *chocolate*, *sh* as in *shop*, *th* as in *thing*).

In our own classrooms, we discovered that blends and digraphs present a special challenge to early readers. We have also found that explicit teaching of blends and digraphs helps children tremendously in their literacy development. As with word families, when children can compare blends and digraphs in new words to words they already know, they'll read with greater confidence and fluency. For instance, if children know that the letters *s* and *h* make the *sh* sound in *shop*, they can more easily read or write *ship*, *shape*, *shoe*, or *shine*.

Since we knew what we needed to focus on—blends and digraphs—we searched for appropriate materials. We turned to poetry! In this book, you'll find 40 delightful poems that will help make word study playful and engaging. You can use them to teach specific blends and digraphs, build reading fluency, and improve children's overall literacy skills. Plus…they're great fun!

Shelley Grant
   Kindergarten Teacher,
   The Elias Howe School, P.S. 51
   District 2, Manhattan

Dana Haddad
   Assistant Director of Nursery
   and Lower Division Admissions,
   Horace Mann School, Manhattan

Using This Book

Sharing and studying the poems is easy as 1, 2, 3. Here are the basic steps to follow for any poem:

1. In advance, write the poem on chart paper. You can also enlarge it on a copy machine, or copy it onto an overhead transparency and show it on the overhead projector. You might also copy the page for each child.

2. Read the title and have children predict what the poem may be about. Then read the poem aloud to children, tracking the print as you go. Read the poem again, inviting children to join in when they can. If a word is new to children, invite them to try using the context of the poem to figure it out.

3. Investigate the target blend or digraph. Point out one word in the poem that has that letter combination. As a class, find other words with the blend or digraph. Give children each a copy of page 6, have them fill in the target blend or digraph, and then write the words with that letter combination in the poem. They can write them in the magnifying glass (several poems include only one or two). At the bottom of the page, they can then list all other words in the family that they can think of. (If they each have their own poem page, they can also circle or highlight all the blends or digraphs they find.) Use the lists on page 48 for reference.

40 WONDERFUL BLEND & DIGRAPH POEMS Scholastic Teaching Resources

Letter Detective

I'm looking for words with ⬚ :

_____ _____

_____ _____

_____ _____

_____ _____

_____ _____

_____

Other words with ⬚ :

_____ _____

_____ _____

_____ _____

6

Extending & Enriching the Lessons

There are lots of ways to build on children's understanding of the blends, digraphs, and poems:

- **Children can act out many of the poems.** They may also enjoy making up their own movements to accompany a poem.

- **As you read a poem aloud, invite children to clap** when they hear a word with the target blend or digraph.

- **Write words on index cards and have children sort them by letter combination.** For instance, they can sort words beginning with *bl-* and *cr-* into two different groups.

- **Create a word wall** and display words according to blends or digraphs they feature. You might begin by having children's names ready to put on the word wall and guiding children to notice blends and digraphs. Ask children to decide where the names should go.

- **Record poems on audiotape.** Make copies of the pages and place them at the listening center. Children can listen to the poems as they read along.

- **Have children color in the pictures** on each poem page, or create their own illustration for the poem on a separate sheet of paper.

- **Write each line of a poem on a sentence strip** and have children work in pairs to recreate the sequence of the poem. After the partners reconstruct a poem, they can read it aloud to the group.

- **Bind the poems together and send them home as a poetry book.** You might also put the poems in a folder. At the end of the school year, children will have their own collection of poems for their personal libraries.

- **At home, families can help children find the target blends or digraphs** in books, magazines, or newspapers. They can also help their children look for the different letter combinations in environmental print, for example, on labels in the supermarket or signs on stores.

Brushes

Hair brushes, tooth brushes,
Paint brushes, clothes brushes,
Scrub brushes, tub brushes,
Nobody knows brushes,
Nail brushes, shoe brushes,
Dish brushes, pot brushes
I'm sick of brushing
With goodness knows what brushes.
Quick, but another one!
Wonder what the rush is?
We need to buy a brush
To brush all the brushes!

-Jeff Moss

40 WONDERFUL BLEND & DIGRAPH POEMS   Scholastic Teaching Resources

Brooms

On stormy days
When the wind is high,
Tall trees are brooms
Sweeping the sky.

They swish their branches
In buckets of rain
And swash and sweep it
Blue again.

-Dorothy Aldis

Cheers for Cherry Cake

Gather, children, give a cheer
for the greatest treat made far and near!
Fill your cheeks and chomp and chew,
you'll all get one slice…maybe two!
'Cause today's the day the baker bakes…
her famous chocolate-chip cherry cake!

-Kama Einhorn

Chick, Chick, Chatterman

Chick, chick, chatterman,
How much are your geese?
Chick, chick, chatterman,
Five cents apiece.
Chick, chick, chatterman,
That's too dear.
Chick, chick, chatterman,
Get out of here!

-Traditional

11

The Click Clacker Machine

The Click Clacker Machine
    makes clackers that click.
The clackers click quickly
    but sometimes they stick.
When quick clicking clackers
    are sticking, they crack.
Then the clackers are clickless
    and put in a sack.
Sacked clackers are sent
    to the clicking inspectors
Who all claim to be
    clickless clacker collectors.

-Donna Lugg Pape

12

Clown Class

Little clowns, come along.
It's time for school.
In clown class you'll learn
all the clown rules.

In clown class, please ask
any question at all,
no matter how silly
or off-the-wall.

Can clowns clap for the audience?
Should a clown wear clogs?
Can you climb on a cloud?
Can you juggle with frogs?

Does a clam have claws?
Are the stars made of clay?
Ask silly questions,
and maybe someday...

You'll be a clown teacher!
And give the clown test:
Did you make the class laugh?
That's better than best!

-Kama Einhorn

cl-

13

cr-

Crazy Crying Cats

What's that noise out at the creek?
Crazy crying cats.

If you listen closely
you can hear them speak.
Crazy crying cats.

Now do your best to stay out of their way.
Crazy crying cats.

When they come, they'll be running astray!
Crazy crying cats.

-Ellen Booth Church

40 WONDERFUL BLEND & DIGRAPH POEMS   Scholastic Teaching Resources

There Was a Crooked Man

There was a crooked man
And he walked a crooked mile;
He found a crooked sixpence
Beside a crooked stile;
He bought a crooked cat
And it caught a crooked mouse
And they both lived together
In a wee crooked house.

-Traditional

15

dr-

Dragon Dream

In my dreamy little dream,
a dragon wore a dress.
I drove her in my jeep.
She really was impressed!

I dragged her to the grocery store,
she didn't make a peep.
She gave a little dragon sigh,
and drifted off to sleep.

-Kama Einhorn

16

Raindrops

rain
drops
drip
down
all
day
long.

drip down,
slip down,
splashing out their song.

thunder-crashing
splishing
splashing,
slipping,
dripping,

raining down
their rainy
raindrop
song.

-Helen H. Moore

17

A Flea and a Fly in a Flue

A flea and a fly in a flue
Were imprisoned, so what could they do?
Said the fly, "Let us flee."
Said the flea, "Let us fly."
So they flew through a flaw in the flue.

-Traditional

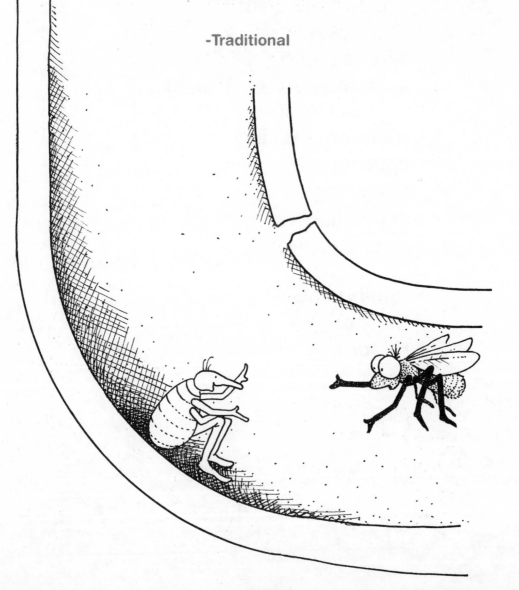

If I Could Fly

If I could fly,
I'd flap these arms.
I'd flap right off the ground.
I'd join a flock of geese up high,
and flip and float around.
And when I'd flown for many miles,
I'd flop down in my nest,
and rest my tired little wings,
and take a nice long rest.

-Kama Einhorn

19

Grandma's Going to the Grocery Store

Grandma's going to the grocery store. 1, 2, 3, 4.
Grandma's going to the grocery store. 1, 2, 3, 4.
Who's going? Grandma's going.
Where's she going? To the grocery store. 1, 2, 3, 4.
When's she going? At a quarter after four. 1, 2, 3, 4.
What's she going to buy at the grocery store? 1, 2, 3, 4.
What's she going to buy at the grocery store? 1, 2, 3, 4.
A loaf of bread, a bottle of milk,
a big bag of cookies and a little can of peas.
Grandma's going to the grocery store. 1, 2, 3, 4.

-Naomi Baltuck

40 WONDERFUL BLEND & DIGRAPH POEMS   Scholastic Teaching Resources

Grasshopper Green

Grasshopper green
Too quick to be seen
Jump like a Mexican jumpity bean!

Grasshopper high
Grasshopper low
Over my basket of berries you go!

Grasshopper low
Grasshopper high
Watch it or you will end up in a pie!

-Nancy Dingman Watson

70 WONDERFUL WORD FAMILY POEMS Scholastic Professional Books

Eletelephony

Once there was an elephant,
Who tried to use the telephant—
No! No! I mean an elephone
Who tried to use the telephone—
(Dear me! I am not certain quite
That even now I've got it right.)

However it was, he got his trunk
Entangled in the telephunk;
The more he tried to get it free,
The louder buzzed the telephee—
(I fear I'd better drop the song
Of elephop and telephong!)

-Laura E. Richards

Phoebe's Phase

My older sister Phoebe
is going through a phase.
Buying makeup at the pharmacy's
just part of her new craze.
She's on the phone all night long.
Rock stars' photos on her wall.
I do think that teenagers
are the strangest things of all.

-Kama Einhorn

23

She Sells Seashells

She sells seashells
by the seashore.
The shells that she sells
are seashells, I'm sure.
So if she sells seashells
by the seashore,
I'm sure that the shells
are seashore shells.

-Traditional

Shirley Shepherd

Shirley Shepherd counted sheep:
one sheep two sheep three sheep four,
shuffling through her bedroom door.
And when she drifted off to sleep,
she dreamed of those four shaggy sheep:
one sheep two sheep three sheep four,
eating shortcake off her floor!

-Brook Pieri

Skipping

The high skip,
The sly skip,
The skip like a feather.
The long skip,
The strong skip,
The skip all together.
The slow skip,
The toe skip,
The skip double-double.
The fast skip,
The last skip,
The skip against trouble!

-Eleanor Farjeon

sk-

Skyscraper

Skyscraper, skyscraper,
Scrape me some sky:
Tickle the sun
While the stars go by.

Tickle the stars
While the sun's climbing high,
Then skyscraper, skyscraper,
Scrape me some sky.

-Dennis Lee

27

Icy

I slip and I slide
On the slippery ice;
I skid and I glide—
Oh, isn't it nice
To lie on your tummy
And slither and skim
On the slick crust of snow
Where you skid as you swim?

-Rhoda W. Bacmeister

The Slow, Sleepy Sloth

There's a rainforest creature you really should meet.
She's got three toes on each of her feet.
Her name is another word for slow.
She's the sleepiest creature I ever did know.
Slumbers all day and slumbers all night,
Asleep in the treetops, way out of sight.
Sleep tightly, sweet sloth,
And know this is true:
Sometimes we all feel exactly like you!

-Kama Einhorn

40 WONDERFUL BLEND & DIGRAPH POEMS   Scholastic Teaching Resources

Snuggles the Snake

A snail can't snuggle
because of its shell.
But Snuggles the Snake
can snuggle quite well.
So if you make friends
with Snuggles the Snake,
here's some advice
you really should take.
She'll try to curl up
and snuggle with you
(this snake loves to cuddle,
surprising but true)
and nuzzle and sniffle
and cuddle and snore,
and if you refuse—
she'll sniffle some more!

-Kama Einhorn

30

The Snail

**Quietly sneaking
through the garden,
the tiny snail
delicately snips off
a piece of leaf,
then moves on a silvery trail
to find another
leafy snack.**

-Shelley Grant

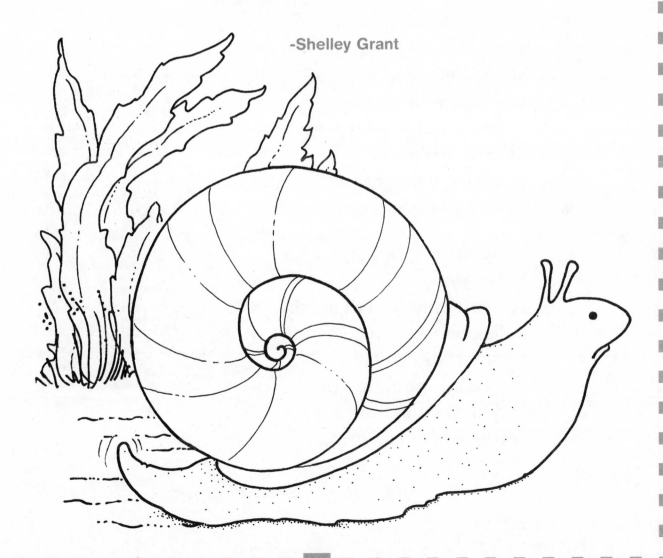

Spaghetti! Spaghetti!

Spaghetti! spaghetti!
you're wonderful stuff,
I love you, spaghetti,
I can't get enough.
You're covered with sauce
and you're sprinkled with cheese,
spaghetti! spaghetti!
oh, give me some please.

Spaghetti! spaghetti!
piled high in a mound,
you wiggle, you wriggle,
you squiggle around.
There's slurpy spaghetti
all over my plate,
spaghetti! spaghetti!
I think you are great.

Spaghetti! spaghetti!
I love you a lot,
you're slishy, you're sloshy,
delicious and hot.
I gobble you down
oh, I can't get enough,
spaghetti! spaghetti!
you're wonderful stuff.

-Jack Prelutsky

Spin, Spider, Spin!

Spin, spider, spin!
Spin your web round and wide.
Spin your silky web with pride.
Greet the guests who come inside.
Spin, spider, spin.

-Meish Goldish

33

Showers

Squelch and squirt and squiggle,
Drizzle and drip and drain—
Such a lot of water
Comes down with the rain!

-Marchette Chute

A Squirmy Squid

A squirmy squid is squiggling.
Squids always write with ink.
She squirms because she's giggling,
which makes it hard to think.
The giggling turns to squealing,
the squealing turns to squawks.
The squawking wakes the walrus,
who was sleeping on the rocks.
The walrus cries "Who's squeaking?"
"I'm down here!" squeaks the squid.
"Please, help me finish up this poem!"
and so the walrus did.

-Jed Miller

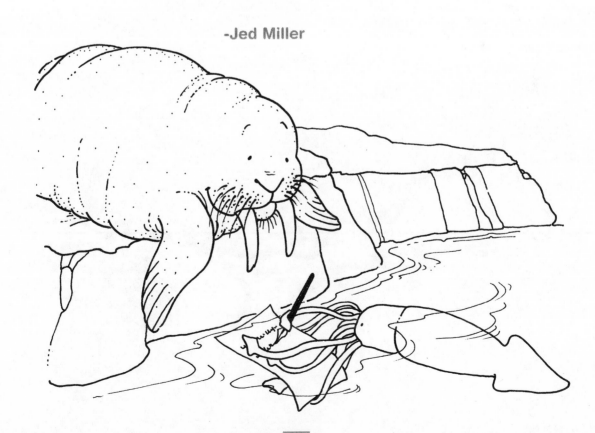

35

Rhyme

I like to see a thunder storm,
    A dunder storm,
        A blunder storm,
I like to see it, black and slow,
Come stumbling down the hills.

I like to hear a thunder storm,
    A plunder storm,
        A wonder storm,
Roar loudly at our little house
And shake the window sills!

-Elizabeth Coatsworth

Stella's Seed

Stella found a seed.
She planted it.
She watered it.
She hoped that it would grow.
Every day,
she stopped by the garden.
Every day,
she stood in the sun.
Stella watched
as her seed grew
into a plant with a stem
that grew into
a sunflower.

-Shelley Grant

In the Park

In the park I swing and sway
on such a sweltering summer day!
A swarm of bees swoops down to play,
They buzz and swarm—
I run away!

-Brook Pieri

My Sweet

**Swallow your snowpeas please,
my sweet.
Swing swiftly on the swivel swing,
little darling.
Swirl through the swishing leaves,
and swim in the sweltering sun,
my sweetest sweet
sugary bun.**

-Brook Pieri

Mice

I think mice
Are rather nice.
Their tails are long,
Their faces small,
They haven't any
Chins at all.
Their ears are pink,
Their teeth are white,
They run about
The house at night.
They nibble things
They shouldn't touch
And no one seems
To like them much.

But I think mice
Are nice.

-Rose Fyleman

There's a Hole in the Bucket

There's a hole in the bucket,
dear Theo, dear Theo,
There's a hole in the bucket,
dear Theo, a hole!

Then fix it, dear Thelma,
dear Thelma, dear Thelma.
Then fix it, dear Thelma,
dear Thelma, fix it!

With what shall I fix it,
dear Theo, dear Theo?
With what shall I fix it,
dear Theo, with what?

With straw then, dear Thelma,
dear Thelma, dear Thelma.
With straw then, dear Thelma,
dear Thelma, with straw!

-Traditional

41

Troll Pal

You may think trolls are trouble,
but that's simply not true.
I have a little troll friend.
Let me tell you.

He lives in a tree
down a trail near my home.
He's sweet (but speaks only
a language called Gnome).

I try to be nice—
I bring treats on a tray.
He's starting to trust me.
He wants me to stay!

-Kama Einhorn

42

Trick or Treat

Off to trick or treat we go.
Trying to scare everyone we know.
Tracy and I and my dog Troy
(who really is such a nice boy),
traveling along a treacherous trail.
"This trio's trouble!" the neighbors wail.

-Kama Einhorn

43

Twins

I think it would be
Lots of fun,
If I were two
Instead of one.

I'd never be lonely
Outdoors or in,
For wherever I'd go
Would go my twin.

On birthdays Mother
Would always bake
Two—not one
Big birthday cakes.

At night there'd be
Two soft little beds,
And two soft pillows
For two sleepyheads.

Oh, everything would be
Doubly nice,
If I could only
Be me twice!

-Jean Brabham McKinney

tw-

Twin Town

In Twin Town you'll find:
Twelve twins twirling twigs.
Twenty twins twisting.
Twin ladies in wigs.

Twin bluebirds tweeting.
Stars twinkling in twos.
You'll see everything twice—
even twin kangaroos!

-Kama Einhorn

45

What Is Pink?

What is pink? A rose is pink
By the fountain's brink.
What is red? A poppy's red
In its barley bed.
What is blue? The sky is blue
Where the clouds float through.
What is white? A swan is white
Sailing in the light.
What is yellow? Pears are yellow,
Rich and ripe and mellow.
What is green? The grass is green,
With small flowers between.
What is violet? Clouds are violet
In the summer twilight.
What is orange? Why, an orange,
Just an orange!

-Christina Rossetti

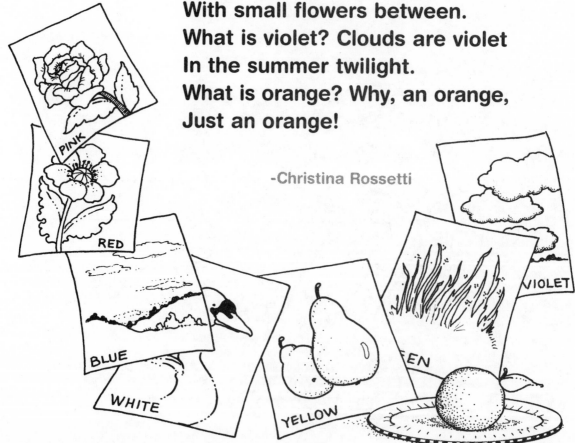

40 WONDERFUL BLEND & DIGRAPH POEMS Scholastic Teaching Resources

White Sheep

White sheep, white sheep
On a blue hill.
When the wind stops
You all stand still.
When the wind blows
You walk away slow.
White sheep, white sheep,
Where did you go?

-Christina Rossetti

BLEND & DIGRAPH WORD LISTS

BR-	CH-	CL-	DR-	GR-	SH	SL-	SP-	ST-	SW-	TR-
brace	chain	clack	drab	grab	shabby	slab	space	stable	swallow	trace
brad	chair	claim	draft	grace	shack	slack	span	stack	swam	track
braid	chalk	clam	drag	grade	shade	slam	spare	stadium	swamp	trade
brain	chalkboard	clamp	dragon	graft	shadow	slant	spark	staff	swan	trail
braise	challenge	clan	drain	grain	shag	slap	spat	stage	swap	train
brake	chamber	clank	drake	gram	shake	slate	speak	stain	swarm	tramp
bran	champ	clap	drank	grand	shall	sled	spear	stair	swat	trap
branch	champion	clarinet	drape	grandfather	shame	sleek	speck	stake	swatch	trash
brand	chance	clash	draw	grandmother	shampoo	sleep	speech	stale	sway	tray
brass	change	clasp	dread	grant	shamrock	sleepy	speed	stalk	sweat	tread
brat	channel	class	dream	grape	shape	sleet	spell	stall	sweater	treat
brave	chant	classroom	dress	graph	share	slept	spend	stamp	sweep	tree
brawl	chap	clay	drew	grasp	shark	slice	spent	stand	sweet	trek
bray	chapter	clean	drift	grass	sharp	slick	spike	staple	sweeten	tribe
bread	charcoal	clear	drill	grasshopper	shatter	slid	spill	stapler	swell	trick
break	charge	clench	drink	grate	shave	slide	spin	star	swept	trim
breathe	charm	clerk	drip	grave	shawl	slight	spine	starch	swerve	trip
breeze	chart	clever	drive	gravity	she	slim	spire	stare	swift	troll
brew	chase	cliff	droop	gravy	shed	slime	spirit	starfish	swim	tromp
brick	chat	climate	drug	gray	sheep	sling	spoil	start	swine	trot
bride	chatter	climb	drum	graze	sheet	slip	spoke	starve	swing	trouble
bridge	cheap	clinic	dry	grease	shell	slipper	sponge	state	swish	trough
bright	cheat	clink		great	shelf	slit	spoon	station	switch	trout
brim	check	clip		greed	shelter	slope	sport	stationery	swollen	truck
bring	checker	clock	**FL-**	green	shock	slot	spur	statue	swoop	true
brisk	cheek	clog	flag	greet	shoe	slow	spy	stay		truly
broad	cheer	close	flake	grew	shoot	slowly		steady		trumpet
broil	cheerful	cloth	flame	grid	shop	slug		steak	**TH-**	trunk
broke	cheese	clothes	flap	grill	shore	slump	**SQU-**	steal	than	trust
bronco	cheeseburger	cloud	flare	grim	short	slush	square	steam	thank	truth
bronze	cheetah	clove	flash	grime	should	sly	squash	steel	that	try
brood	cherry	clown	flashlight	grin	shoulder		squat	steep	thaw	
brook	chess	club	flat	grind	shove		squeak	steer	the	**TW-**
broom	chest	cluck	flaw	grip	shovel	**SN-**	squeal	stem	theater	tweed
broth	chestnut	clue	flea	grit	show	snack	squeeze	step	their	tweet
brother	chew	clump	fleck	groan	shower	snag	squid	stereo	them	tweezers
brought	chick	clumsy	fleet	groceries	shuffle	snail	squint	stew	theme	twelve
brown	chicken	cluster	flesh	groom	shush	snake	squirm	stick	then	twenty
browse	chief	clutch	flew	grouch	shut	snap	squirrel	sticky	there	twice
bruise	child	clutter	flex	ground	shutter	snare	squirt	stiff	thermometer	twig
brush	children		flick	group	shy	snarl	squish	still	they	twin
	chili		flight	grow		snatch		stilt	thick	twine
	chill	**CR-**	fling	growl	**SK-**	sneak		sting	thief	twinkle
	chilly	crab	flint	grown	skate	sneeze		stingy	thigh	twirl
	chime	crack	flip	grub	sketch	sniff		stink	thing	twist
	chimp	cradle	float	grudge	ski	snip		stir	think	
	chimney	craft	flock	gruff	skid	snob		stirrup	thin	**WH-**
	China	crane	flood	grump	skill	snoop		stitch	third	whack
	chin	crash	floor		skillet	snore		stock	thirst	whale
	chip	crawl	flop		skin	snout		stocking	thirteen	what
	chirp	crayon	floss	**PH-**	skip	snow		stomach	thirty	wheat
	chocolate	crazy	flour	pharmacy	skirt	snug		stone	thorn	wheel
	choke	creek	flow	phase	skit	snuggle		stool	those	when
	chomp	creep	flower	phone	skull			stoop	thought	where
	choose	crib	flu	pheasant	skunk			stop	thousand	whether
	chop	cricket	fluff	philip	sky			store	thumb	which
	chopstick	cried	fluid	Philadelphia				storm	thump	whiff
	chow	croak	fluke	philosophy				story	thunder	while
	chowder	crook	flush	phobia				stove		whim
	chubby	crop	flute	phonics				style		whimper
	chug	cross	fly	phony						whine
	chunky	crow		photo						whip
		crowd		phrase						whirl
		crown								whisker
		crumb								whisper
		crunch								whistle
		crust								white
		cry								who
										whole

40 WONDERFUL BLEND & DIGRAPH POEMS Scholastic Teaching Resources